W9-AYQ-930

Festivals

My
Rosh Hashanah

Monica Hughes

Chicago, Illinois

© 2004 Raintree
Published by Raintree, a division of Reed Elsevier, Inc.
Chicago, Illinois
Customer Service 888-363-4266
Visit our website at www.raintreelibrary.com

Printed and bound in the United States at Lake Book Manufacturing, Inc.
07 06 05 04 03
10 9 8 7 6 5 4 3 2 1

Library of Congress Cataloging-in-Publication Data:
Hughes, Monica.
  My Rosh Hashanah / Monica Hughes.
     p. cm. -- (Festivals)
Summary: Illustrations and simple text describe how one family
celebrates Rosh Hashanah.
Includes bibliographical references and index.
  ISBN 1-4109-0641-8 (library binding) -- ISBN 1-4109-0667-1 (pbk.)
  1. Rosh ha-Shanah--Juvenile literature. [1. Rosh ha-Shanah. 2.
Holidays.] I. Title. II. Series: Hughes, Monica. Festivals.
  BM695.N5H84 2003
  296.4'315--dc21
                    5581   2003010857

Acknowledgments
The Publishers would like to thank Chris Schwarz and Corbis/Richard T. Nowitz for permission to reproduce photographs.

Cover photograph of the children learning about Abraham and Isaac, reproduced with permission of Chris Schwarz.

Every effort has been made to contact copyright holders of any material reproduced in this book.
Any omissions will be rectified in subsequent printings if notice is given to the publishers.

Some words are shown in bold, **like this.** You can find out
what they mean by looking in the glossary on page 24.

Contents

Happy New Year!

Rosh Hashanah is the Jewish New Year.

We get New Year's cards from our friends.

Getting Ready for Rosh Hashanah

Our **rabbi** teaches us about Rosh Hashanah.

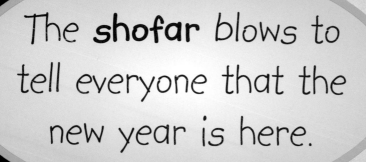

The **shofar** blows to tell everyone that the new year is here.

shofar

We try to blow the shofar, too.

7

Special Treats

We help make challah.

I can help Mom with the honey cake, too.

9

Dressing Up

My dad and I wear **kippot**.

In **synagogues** around the world, the shofar blows.

13

A Special Meal

We are going to eat a special meal.
I will put the **challah** on the table.

This is our **Rosh Hashanah** meal.

Can you find the challah?

Rosh Hashanah Blessings

Mom lights the candles.

We each take one sip of sweet wine.

17

Family and Friends

We share our meal with our family and friends.

New Year's Sweets

We will eat apples dipped in sweet honey.
We will eat sweet honey cake.

We hope these sweet treats will bring us a sweet year.

The Second Day

We take a walk by the water.

We bring some **challah**.

We throw pieces of challah into the water.
The water will carry it away.

23

Glossary

challah (You say HAH-luh.) sweet bread that is usually braided. At Rosh it may be round and may have raisins in it.

kippot (You say KIP-puht; one is a KIP-uh.) small, round cap that Jewish boys and men wear to cover their heads

rabbi (You say RABB-eye.) person who can lead Jewish worship services. Rabbi means "teacher."

Rosh Hashanah (You say ROSH ha-SHAH-nuh.) Jewish celebration of the New Year that takes place each fall in September or October. There are two days of Rosh Hashanah.

shofar (You say SHOW-fahr.) horn that is made out of the horn of a big sheep called a ram

synagogue (You say SINN-uh-gog.) place where Jewish people hold worship services

Index